Poems by
Susan Kinsolving
Paintings by
Susan Colgan

Among Flowers

A PANACHE PRESS BOOK
CLARKSON POTTER/PUBLISHERS
NEW YORK

40309

Published by Panache Press, an imprint of Clarkson N. Potter,
Inc., 201 East 50th Street, New York, New York, 10022.
Member of the Crown Publishing Group. Random House, Inc.
New York, Toronto, London, Sydney, Auckland

CLARKSON N. POTTER, POTTER, PANACHE PRESS, and
colophon are trademarks of Clarkson N. Potter, Inc.

Manufactured in China
Design by K. C. Witherell
Library of Congress Cataloging-in-Publication Number: 92–34136
ISBN 0–517–59114–6
10 9 8 7 6 5 4 3 2 1
First Edition

Preceding page, left: *Nasturtiums in Yellow Pot I.*
Preceding page, right: *Nasturtiums in Yellow Pot II.*
Final page: *Willow Cups on Drain Board.*

In this mixed bouquet of art and letters, Susan Kinsolving and Susan Colgan take a fresh look at familiar flowers—and what they see is a garden of delights and surprises. The two share not only first names, but similar sensibilities—to both artists, flowers are not just objects of sublime shape and scent, but evocations of what matters to each.

The voice of poet Susan Kinsolving is modern—sometimes lyrical, sometimes wry, sometimes the purveyor of fascinating fact and fable. In her poems, flowers become metaphors for impressions and memories that touch, amuse, or astonish. Painter Susan Colgan's vivid oils present skillful compositions of flowers with sundries of domesticity or the closer-than-close inspection of single blooms. Whatever the perspective, the paintings celebrate flowers as irreplaceable grace notes and ornaments of living.

In a remarkable synergy, the poems and paintings do double duty—Kinsolving's pointed observations in verse paint word pictures, and Colgan's color-drenched still lifes tell stories. Together, they offer a contemporary collaboration of charm, character, and originality.

NASTURTIUMS IN YELLOW POT III, 21½×30¼ INCHES, OIL/CANVAS, 1989

NOT A STILL LIFE

A mixed bouquet may mediate
among colors and shapes, make
sense of so many sensibilities.
See the nasturtiums fan and
restrain their small flames?
And the zinnia composes a full
circle of kisses and contusions
covered with pink tiers as sweet
peas intimate a sheen of skin.
Where do flowers end and begin?
Ancient and infamous, they swarm
with bees and all allusions
that are alive, blooming and being.

TULIPS IN QUIMPER POT, 28×30 INCHES, OIL/CANVAS, 1991

Tulipomania,
the Wind Trade (1634-37)

When Holland went insane, a tulip bulb replaced
each brain. Speculation soared. Fortunes in florins
would afford merely a bulb. In shrieks, brokers bid
paying dearly for "broken" petals of enflamed streaks.
Merchants offered the moon for one bulbil of Zomerschoon
and called it "sport" when mutations might distort
a Rembrandt's variegation. Everywhere fast money was made
though skeptics said such a "Wind Trade" would never
last, for the goddess Flora and her fools made a folly
of fiscal rules. And each exotic tulip bearing an inflated
price also bore a virus transmitted by lice. When over-
night the crash came, no one dwelt on blight or blame.
Fusing fantasy, finance, and flowers still seemed better
than other worldly powers. Inasmuch, God blest the Dutch.

IN A FIELD OF
BLACK-EYED SUSANS
AN ACROSTIC

Sitting here among so many Susans,
    shoulder high, I ask a simple though

Unlikely question: why is this,
    my namesake flower, not a lily but a daisy?

Susan's a lily straight from her Hebrew root;
    it's even more silly and brute to name

A blossom with the likes of a shiner when
    likelier girls are kept benigner.

No Violet, Iris, or Rose suffers a split lip or
    ever bloodies a nose. Yet something's well-

Suited that our flower can claim, the bright
    spunk needed for so common a name.

COFFEE POT AND WOODEN BOWLS AT MIDDAY, 23×29 INCHES, OIL/CANVAS, 1990

At the Florist

When asked if he wanted
his anthers cut off,
he paused for a moment,
dissembled a cough,

Then mumbled and shrugged
"I'm only a layman . . ."
"But surely" she smiled
"you know about stamens

And all of the grief
that's caused by their spread."
He adjusted his glasses,
"I'm not so well-read . . ."

Lifting a lily
from its cold water urn,
she said "A superbum
from which you can learn."

As she drew the great blossom
close to her bust
she fingered the filament's
lurid red dust.

"You see how a flower
erects its own stigma
though past all reproach
and free of enigma.

It's held by the pistil,
overt and with style
in a coiling of color,
sweet and fertile."

The silence grew, tense
with a cloying perfume.
A hothouse took over
her semifrigid room.

Seeing her body's smooth moves
he felt it his fate.
High on hybrids, he thought
. . . time to cross-pollinate . . .

"What has to be done,"
he gasped "we must do."
She gathered the lilies,
"You'll know when I'm through."

Then stepping beside him
she tended each flower
humming and snipping
till he started to glower.

"Your fervor's just this?
A mere shearing of pollen?!"
"A favor, no fervor.
Don't look so crestfallen."

When she laid the lilies
on a cellophane wrap
she gave his plaid shoulder
a good-ole-boy slap

"Now your garments won't need
to visit the cleaner;
there's no stain in nature
as tough or obscener

Than the anther's satanic
impregnating dust,
those tiny male nuggets
full of tangible lust.

It's been a real pleasure
to fix these for you.
Your lilies are gelded.
What more can I do?"

MEMORABILIA MAGNOLIA

Pierre Magnol to Monticello, Francisco Hernandez to Kew,
Aztecs to Alabama bayou, the panorama of history in these
durable dense leaves is magnificent and immense. American
Indians feared a perfume so intense while Szechwan Chinese
stripped the anise-scented bark for remedies. But long before
butterflies or bees, amid cycad palms, conifers and ferns
as tall as trees, a beetle was the evolutionary link between
pollen and magnolia flowers. Astonishing such powers or
to think that one hundred million years ago, the last
stegosaur tried to eat these pristine petals, but fell extinct
upon its fossilizing feet. Imagine what is nevermore, how
these branches stirred with gigantic mouths and toothed birds.

MAGNOLIAS AGAINST THE SKY, 20×22 INCHES, OIL/CANVAS, 1991

The Humdrum
and the Geranium

By the fire escape or kitchen sink
in engine red or salmon pink, root-
bound in pots with lots of rocks
or left bone-dry in a window box,
they tough it out without disdain
and beautify the most mundane.
Where fancy flowers sense disgrace,
shrivel up, and shun the place,
geraniums thrive. Against asphalt
assaults or rooms of dust, they
survive and bloom as if they must
give the banal their small relief
of bright bud and scalloped leaf.

MY WINDOWSILL ON 89TH STREET, 22×32¼ INCHES, OIL/CANVAS, 1991

NASTURTIUMS, FOXGLOVES, AND SOAPDISH, 12×10 INCHES,
OIL/MASONITE, 1989

BOUQUET, CUT GLASS, TEA INFUSER, 26×26 INCHES,
OIL/CANVAS, 1990

ALLUDING TO DAFFODILS

Remember years ago, a day among our last
when we kept digging in the bed
though it was cold and overcast? Half-
smiling "What might it mean," you asked
"I'm burying King Alfreds while yours are
called Bronze Queen?" I gave a shrug
as you went on, "Pliny said these bulbs
drug, make the body numb. He called Ovid's
myth merely 'meddlesome.'" A long
silence ensued. You shoved your spade along
a string of "naturalizing" lines. I stomped
clumps into the ground and skewed our spring
designs. "Echo died," I finally replied.
"Her curse was endless naming, yet Narcissus
saw himself clearly past all blaming." Why
after decades do I bring this nonsense back?
Perhaps the mind is like an old bulb sack
with dark words waiting to have their day.
When I see yellow waves upon the hills or

a pitcher full of bright jonquils, I feel
an old dismay. For we disguised our poison
as these flowers do in their clear viscosity
and buried love so deep we never realized
its luminosity. When we parted, I wandered
lonely as a cloud, looking for you in any crowd.

DAFFODILS, 28×20 INCHES,
OIL/CANVAS, 1989

SUMMER STUDIO, ANNA'S ROSE, 18×30 INCHES, OIL/CANVAS, 1990

ARIA

One day even the air was insistent, pouring over us
as if the season had extracted its own essence
and we were awash with its scent. The roses opened

to their fullest intimation and we inhaled deeply
though we could not hold a breath for time throbbed
in our veins. We knew our great luck was being

alive together in that extreme lush atmosphere where
fragrance grew emphatic and the moist grass implored us
to fall upon it. When we did, the cultivated allegory

of earth flowered in our flesh and a buried path
of stones led us back, beyond our bones. Wordless,
we could not admit how much we wanted to have a night

so persistent in the same perfume, how we craved
a chance to consummate all the landscapes lost
in dark rooms, all the time imagined by late blooms.

GERTRUDE JEKYLL'S MYOPIA

Entering each flower, her eyes magnified
its pistil, stamen, petal, perianth, and stem
into a magnificence of distinct design.
Her dark pupils, deep in their encircling
irises, studied the flower as form.
Intensifying its splendor, enlarging
its inflorescence, her myopia was a looking-
glass in which the singular blossom grew
big and basic until she turned her glance
away to gain her greater vision. Impressionist
of the garden, she saw the beautiful blur
in which every exactitude was capacious
with pleasure, every affliction was changed
to advantage. Miss Jekyll's retinas were
crystalline with foresight and knowing looks.
Imagine her discernment and voluminosity, planning
three hundred gardens and writing fourteen books.

PARTED CURTAIN, WINTER, 11 5/8 × 8 7/8 INCHES,
OIL/MASONITE, 1991

To a Forced Amaryllis

Nothing sounds more antithetical to "flower"
than "force." Yet presumably, we are forcing
you to flower by these white windows etched
by ice and framed by sills of snow. Somehow
I sense you know it's not the natural season.

Instinct tells you so and your green reason
allows that this clay pot is a tricky garden
plot. Still you're warming up to our coercion
and soon you'll lavish your blossom upon this
freezing day, our sorceress made to conjure May.

BOUQUETS FOR EMILY, 13×7¾ INCHES,
OIL/CANVAS, 1978

DAY LILIES FROM THE OLD HOUSE SITE, 20×30 INCHES, OIL/CANVAS, 1979

An Old Couple
Observes Ipomoea

To hold on, tenacious as bindweed though tentative
as a thin green spiral extending through air, probing
space with the implicit question: Will anything join
here with there? Clinging against time, tendrilous
on a string, strict counterclockwise coils grasp
railings, trellises, rain gutters, any tactility
for fastening. All to end; each glory goes swiftly
in its silent cornet of blue, summery dawn funneling
through to an apex of afternoon and all too soon.
Yet in this culminating twist, there is no further
reach for meaning, morning passes away too fast
for grieving and the vine continues to entwine
whatever's present, as if it were a great design.

BEHIND THE GARAGE, 12×7 INCHES,
OIL/MASONITE, 1991

AUGUST AFTERNOON, 29×20 INCHES,
OIL/CANVAS, 1989–90

AMONG
FLOWERS

Among flowers, the paradisiac dream
seems still a garden plan, its scheme
in hand and almost attainable
as if each blossom unfurled itself
to offer an abbreviated Eden, an ideal
of ease and absolution. Among
flowers, we live graciously again

between the tender grass and bending bough
in a seeming sanctuary away
from the coiling snake of our souls
and the softening fruit of our flesh.
Among flowers, history is buried
in the cultivated bed, pleasure precedes
knowledge, eternity kisses the ephemeral

and earth opens its opulent bouquet
of perennial promise. Among flowers,
we forget both autumn and the fall;
temptation and exaltation are one. As
the petals unfold, a new genesis starts
its story and we hold, however briefly,
innocence and ecstasy like a breath.

SWEET PEAS, BLUE SHADOWS, SCALLOP SHELL, 11¼×10 INCHES,
OIL/MASONITE, 1989

HENRY ECKFORD'S SWEET PEAS

Consider the aesthetic hybridist, a cross
between artist and scientist. See a visionary
like Henry, obsessed with the culinary
pea (and colorful possibility) devoting
each year to the minute administrations
of consecutive mutations. When one day

(whoopee) he creates a frilled, crimped,
and waved beauty. Botanically,
her keels are strong, so's her perfume,
and her rare wings aren't maroon. No
longer a rustic from Sicily, she now
inspires a world society. While Henry

like a god, aroused her from her pod,
and urged against her wild ways
into a new life of four-bloomed
sprays. The Higgins of her floriferous
pride, he took her as his childbride
insisting her sweetness would be glorified.

Hydrangeas
in Autumn

Enduring regrets are sterile florets
left after the blooms, all blushing and blue
succumb to the true season, turn cinnamon
and dun, parched from a pinker past.
Seeing them last in their dry vase without
earth, water, acids, or alums, I wish
for you and how we too were once all
blushing or blue. Curious, survival.
Still, there's no dispute; this shrub will thrive
again, a tribute to its roots, suckers,
and stems. While dry-eyed and without you,
I view this preservation, this bouquet
of come what may, made for a requiem.

RENEE'S FAVORITE BLUE. 20×22 INCHES. OIL/CANVAS. 1991

Eight Notes
on the Owlpen Delphiniums

1.

Countess Cowley lacks stamina as does Tiger Tim
regardless of whose bed they're in.

2.

Lay down a mixture on a stone. Wet caster sugar.
Grind plaster of Paris powder. Add mealy bone.

3.

Blue Gown and Sensation reliably stay, even black
rot cannot wilt them away.

4.

Leather jacket, wireworm, millipede, earwig, and
cuckoo-spit all take a turn. Spray potassium
sulphur, as on the greenfly. All will die.

5.

Mrs. Foster Cunliffe is best described as one not
to hide. She's a double! But Lady Bath is regular
as ranunculus and that's her trouble.

6.

True relatives come from afar. Cashmirianum from
Kashmir. Elatum from England. The Afghan from Zalil.
Grandiflorum from Siberia, but in the family still.

7.

The column widened to a pyramid shape beginning in 1908,
with Smoke of War. Then came Millicent Blackmore.

8.

One ton of horse dung has only fourteen pounds of nitrate.
Poultry, pig, sheep, and cow have a superior rate.

DELPHINIUMS IN THE DARK, 26×30 INCHES, OIL/CANVAS, 1989

GLOSSES ON THE POEMS

*Sometimes a poet will offer a brief explanation adding further
meaning to a poem. In the parlance of poetry, such an explanation is called a gloss.*

TULIPOMANIA, THE WIND TRADE (1634–37)

Holland's economy in the 1630s went wild as a wind over tulips, then crashed. Connoisseurs of exotic fringes, flames, streaks, and stripes in the flower invested and lost fortures in a single bulb or tiny bulbil. These floral novelties called "sports" or "breaks" were the result of a virus infecting the bulb. Today X rays scramble tulip genetics to achieve similar effects on the tulip.

IN A FIELD OF BLACK-EYED SUSANS

The name Susan originated with the Hebrew word *Shoshannah*, meaning lily. In 2872 B.C., an Iranian inscription referred to the Semitic city of Susa, The Lilies; however, a black-eyed Susan is a yellow daisy coneflower found in the bottomlands throughout America,

AT THE FLORIST

Lest one forget, flowers are the sexual component of plants. At the center of the lily is the pistil, composed of ovary, stigma, and style. Less loaded with puns are the surrounding six stamens; these male organs composed of anthers and filaments produce pollen. Florists trim them because the dusty orange anthers stain both clothes and petals, if not the bees' knees.

MEMORABILIA MAGNOLIA

History and prehistory are full of magnolias. Francisco Hernandez studied their medicinal uses among the Aztecs. In the next century, they were named after botanist Pierre Magnol and written about by Thomas Jefferson, but most amazing is their early evolution. Beetles fed on the sugary stigmas as big white buttery petals gradually developed and were devoured by dinosaurs.

ALLUDING TO DAFFODILS

When Ovid offered a mythical origin for the narcissus, Pliny the Elder wrote a caustic scientific rebuttal, suspecting the bulb and slimy inner stalk to be toxic. He was correct and gardeners know that animals will avoid the poisonous alkaloids. In Ovid's myth, Narcissus ignores Echo with his self-absorption until she is diminished to only a voice repeating his name. A few words of the poem are also repeated—and Wordsworth's.

GERTRUDE JEKYLL'S MYOPIA

At the turn of the century, Gertrude Jekyll turned away from painting and embroidery due to her extreme and progressive myopia. Her impairment influenced her garden style. Textural and impressionistic, her artistry and energy made her one of England's greatest garden designers.

TO A FORCED AMARYLLIS

"Forcing" is the disagreeable term applied to the indoor techniques that awaken bulbs earlier than they would outdoors. This process, popular since Victorian times, exhausts the bulb so that it will not bloom again.

AN OLD COUPLE OBSERVES IPOMOEA

The genus of morning glories, *Ipomoea*, comes from the Greek "resembling bindweed" or "a worm." English countryside gardeners call the flower "life of man" because it buds, blooms, and wilts all in a day. Its tendrils confound scientists by turning strictly counterclockwise.

AMONG FLOWERS

Ancient Persians called their gardens "pardez." Paradise in many cultures has its vestige in the garden, the only earthly place ideal enough for the gods. Eden alludes to this concept.

HENRY ECKFORD'S SWEET PEAS

In Sicily in 1700, small maroon wildflowers resembling those of edible peas were recorded as having exceptionally sweet perfume. Henry Eckford, "the father of the sweet pea," meticulously cross-fertilized this modest flower with his "Prima Donna" into "Grandifloras" of colorful variety. The "keel" of a sweet pea is the join between the "wings," or two petals, all enlarged through Eckford's long efforts.

HYDRANGEAS IN AUTUMN

The big colorful clusters of hydrangeas are sterile and can be preserved as dry brown bouquets. A hardy shrub, the hydrangea propagates easily, especially by dividing its underground branches, known to gardeners as "suckers." Adding acids or alums to the soil's pH level can change the color of the blooms.

EIGHT NOTES ON THE OWLPEN DELPHINIUMS

At Owlpen in Cheshire, John Leeming devoted his great gardens to delphiniums. In 1931 he published *The Book of the Delphinium*, a charming slender volume full of sound advice and earnest opinion. Hybrids named for countesses and ladies have their faults noted while dung is described with respectful detail.

Susan Kinsolving is grateful to the Corporation of Yaddo and the Ragdale Foundation. Susan Colgan would like to thank photographers Kevin Thomas, Tony Mysak, and Thomas S. Bersten, along with the collectors who kindly allowed their paintings to be reproduced: Edith Iglaer Daly for *Parted Curtain, Winter;* Gretchen Graef for *Coffee Pot and Wooden Bowls at Midday;* Elizabeth Grossman for *Daffodils;* Marika and Lewis Hahn for *Nasturtiums in Yellow Pot III;* Jamie Stern and Jeffrey Weiner for *Delphiniums in the Dark;* Diana Swoyer for *August Afternoon.* Both poet and painter thank Lindsey Crittenden, Howard Klein, and Joy Sikorski of Potter—and Geraldine Stutz for her vision, insight, and determination.